Ce volume,
publié aux Éditions Les Belles Lettres,
a été achevé d'imprimer
en mars 2026
sur les presses
de Présence Graphique
37260 Monts, France

Composition et mise en pages :
IGS-CP à L'Isle-d'Espagnac (16)

N° d'édition : 11497
N° d'impression : 032683899
Dépôt légal : janvier 2022

PRAISE FOR *A Geography That*

"We are nowhere and everywhere in Carla Sofia Ferreira's *A Geography That Does Not Hurt Us*. But never lost. The certainty of Ferreira's uncertainty on home and the heart makes a map for those who know life is 'a fretwork of fragments' we navigate by gut and guile. Both ode and elegy to all the liminal spaces we carry in—and outside—our body, *A Geography That Does Not Hurt Us* transcends time and place to offer a politic on what it means to be both American and not, woman/almost, descendant and maverick, fado and fiction. Lush and fearless, these poems urge us to unbind memory with pain and pleasure, 'to love with both hands and eyes closed what is already leaving . . .' but ultimately stays through word."

—MARINA CARREIRA, author of *Save the Bathwater*

"Joining her practices to the practices of her elders, Carla Sofia Ferreira's poems are an intricately woven work of memory, loss, and transience. I read *A Geography That Does Not Hurt Us* as an extended gesture that emerges out of the work of her beloveds. With her language, she is beside them, washing the streets, pulling detail through the needle with steadfast attention and care. Her language full of grandmother, full of window, light streaming through the window. In this way, these tender poems work to 'dwell in every possibility of place.' Each one a small miracle."

—ARACELIS GIRMAY, author of *The Black Maria*

"Carla Sofia Ferreira is writing from a place not listed on maps or star charts, but imprinted in those untamable regions; the heart, the spirit, the soul. Traveling through odes, fados, and elegies, the poetry in *A Geography That Does Not Hurt Us* is a compass to that very place. A topography and arrangement of deep feeling, deep song, and meditation. The kind that inspires awe, melancolía and sensual lyric music. Ferreira writes, 'This, I think, is my fado: / to love afternoons turned into morning, and / to love with both hands and eyes closed what is already leaving me.' A welcome collection, for a world in need of less hurt."

—ROBERTO CARLOS GARCIA, *What Can I Tell You?*

A GEOGRAPHY THAT DOES NOT HURT US

RIVER RIVER BOOKS *Durham, North Carolina*

CARLA SOFIA FERREIRA

Published in the United States of America

Library of Congress Cataloging-in-Publication Data
Ferreira, Carla Sofia, 1990–
A Geography That Does Not Hurt Us / Carla Sofia Ferreira.
ISBN-13: 979-8-9881378-3-2
Subjects: LCSH: Portuguese Literature; Immigrant Literature; The Ironbound; Women Writers.
LCGFT: Poetry.
Library of Congress Control Number: 2023943700

Cover and interior design by Alban Fischer
Portuguese tiles on cover photographed by Carla Sofia Ferreira

RIVER RIVER BOOKS
10 Linganore Place
Durham, NC 27707

www.RiverRiverBooks.org

Para a minha avó, Domingas Luisa Cunha Fonseca,
com saudade eterna da tua neta—
até 'manhã, se Deus quiser.

CONTENTS

Let this fold-out map from an old geography
book be the only distance.

—ARACELIS GIRMAY

NOTICE

What I keep most from the tree
that has been cut down is how
its roots remain in place to cling
to the earth; they could go anywhere
now, but they stay and they are not
biding their time—they make a point
of holding on to the ground, and they teach
the art of permanence. Above them, birds fly.

I. DEPARTURES

I thought that the things I loved

were places I could always go back to

but the spaces between things become places themselves

and threaten to swallow me whole.

—GREGORY KAN

HEARSAY

They say in Avignon people dance on the bridge
that was either unfinished or fell apart—
no one remembers those folk stories anymore.

Two professors stood in line to dispense
their trays and one gray beard said to the other,
"I advised the young ladies in my class to never
marry on the promise of reform. You must change
the man before you take him." When I walked
back to the dormitory, I thought of my grandmother
knitting lace when the afternoon hunched over
to listen to her intricate pattern, the clicking
of her needles. She has such a knack for consistency
and small detail.

It was a city of walls. A sacred city
rendered blasphemous with graffiti on its
walls and pigeons pecking bits of falafel scattered
on its streets. Six weeks with those walls, I never once made
it to the bridge; we thought of it; we let it go.

The Rhône passes through the city and lets
the talk of its pedestrians and their parables enter.

Our geography is no stranger to reformation.
We write over histories.
Some are unfinished or they fall apart.

ELEGY FOR CERTAINTY

Here is to the neat edges
of my index cards
arranged in piles and the careful
placement of my mechanical pencils,
to a certain height my shoulders
once achieved when I would sit
before my desk.

Here is to a time before restless
walks to the river.
This is a remembrance
of my reckless ease,
my simple knowing,
the way I could count
on a calendar or a person
and not ask but know.

There was a time
of honey poured into tea
as I would crush lemon
at the bottom of a mug
placed on top of my mother's
wooden kitchen table
beneath the antique clock,
swirl the seeds around
until midnight
and everything
was known.

ODE TO A SHARED LANGUAGE

You taught me the words,
    brought them to me like small pebbles
from your father's land,
    a motherland you had never seen—
placed them on my tongue like the host,
    a communion dissolving beneath the surface.

Each tripping syllable,
    tiny liaison between vowel and consonant,
what offerings you brought me.
    Hungry for new vocabulary,
the words tasted like all the honey and wine
    dreamt of in gospel and rumors.

        I am forgetting them now.
        I have been forgetting them for a while now,
        you should know.

    The stress and the break—
whatever words may once have crossed
    the Mediterranean or a deeper body
of water
    I am losing—what little grace
this sacrament leaves me.

ELEGY FOR RHYME

What I keep now is your silence.

The way you left without asking
has kept me wondering
what it was that kept you with me for so long.

You made it easy,
gave me structure and form—
                                        a style.
Each bit of you acting
like a refracted mirror,
reflecting what I could not see
but could only imitate.

The way you danced
made me shake.

No longer here,
I think of you and that music
you liked to play,
letting me sing in a rhythm I did not measure
words to a song I had not learned.

The way you left me
I cannot remember.
Simply *there* and *here* intermixed,
you filled my air like breathing.

RANSOM NOTE FOUND INSIDE A PASSPORT

—after Sandra Simonds

I lived with no regrets
          in a time of uneven promises
                    spinning broken glass
its faceted light refracted—
          fractured and lost.

                    I lived in a time of no continuity,
in minutes robbed from a borrowed hourglass.
          I tiptoed in someone else's midnight dream,
                    miscounting the seconds
to my own slumber.

          I lived with a sense of seeing forward,
                    crafting a stolen time in an odd and delicate fashion
like the sky blue paper cranes
          we once saw in the movie I wish we had never seen.

                    I lived with the promise of a love
that spoke only too bravely and too softly at once.

          I lived in a land of two-way bus tickets
                    the not knowing of arrivals and
the darkness of evening come too soon
          the warm light of the third floor apartment
                    of the old red brick building above the long
standing funeral home.

With intricate steps I moved
across marble floors that were not mine at all, not once.

I lived in wings between curtain and stage
rain-soaked rafters in the house under construction
the checkerboard blanket across the olive green
worn recliner and glances from train windows
and walks down escalators.

I lived in beat with the melodies of the old piano

as the nun sang to us and the way that sad song would follow me round
but does not seem to see me anymore.

I lived, but only for a while
here.

ONE NIGHT

"Home is the place where, when you have to go there,
They have to take you in."
—ROBERT FROST

I once had the ability to grasp my Novembers
separate from my Marches and
calendars did not hang on the wire
like lost socks left out on the laundry line.

When the world was smaller,
I could see my life through a glass bottle.

Thoughtful, I walked down a dark street
near the first hour of the next day with the words
home and *go* on my mind
and oddly, I walked to the brick building that
called me, let me enter, but did not let me in.
It was a cold walk back down its ramp.

What I could not hold from that night
was all I could take with me.
I have reached no point of deep reflection—
the river has been here longer than I have
and its waters are heavy.
I have only climbed the ramps outside buildings
and staircases which lead up in endless succession
while my hands clasp the rails tightly.

The unclasping of a bracelet is such a small thing
in a world not seen through a glass bottle
and I am uncertain about the rules, braids undone.

I walked to the place that calls my name
but it has forgotten the grip of my hands.

It was a cold night
and I had no place to go
but to where they could not take me in.

OPEN LETTER TO THE BOSTON BLIZZARD

Dear Blizzard:
where I am not   , I waited for you last year
in every inch of sunshine
that greeted Cambridge
in bitter cold, frosted air
bleeding the thin cuticles
of my chapped hands holding library books. And now
you've come
and I
am not there.

Though I've promised my friend that this night
would be the one in which I would finally write a poem about
sex and calculators, I find myself writing to you instead:
the sweet snow that
never fell in feet outside
my window, and oh,
that bitter want to dive knee deep
        into piles and piles of you in the hush
                that only snow can bring to a courtyard.

On the other side of the Atlantic,
my mind wanders, following
each of your snowflakes
freewheeling down Mount Auburn,
down Mill Street, down each street,
each quiet alley. I imagine
you skating along the breadth

of the Charles as you call the city
into slumber, and you leave me here:

Sincerely,
hibernating: desire as transparent and thin
as paper snowflakes cut with shaky hands and clumsy scissors.

IN APRIL

Rather I shall remember you when the small courtyard
is covered in snow and the night is filled with silence
placed beneath the tent of sky—you will be
like the flower I first stole from the branches

of the magnolia tree, bursting with pink and violet and white
waxen petals so violently pulsing with earthly life;
that freshness of crushed flower enters the air mixing
with the sweat of dancers' hands and midspring humidity.

So shall I remember you, being gone, the blue
of your bright gaze, the warmth of your palm's surface
held in my hand for one still minute and then let go,
softly like the magnolia that could not stay, but lingered,

bringing with it the memory of every spring—
short lasting and crisply new.

ODE TO THE TREES IN BRANCH BROOK PARK

You are alone at morning
          and it breaks you
                    to grow into
what we have expected. No stranger
          walks these paths
                    late at night. Perhaps even the ghost
                              bride has taken
to haunting other grounds.
          Wary pedestrians
                    arrive to see
                         how the blossoms come
to you how only gentle lovers
          and spring can come.
                    To them, you,
                         tender trees, speak
sleeping adolescence:
          you sing evening
                         songs to them.
                              The stone cathedral
                    watches you
while cars drive
          by, letting the radio voice touch the tips
                    of your branches. Once bent with snow,
                                        you sway nearing summer.

Now is the new time.

Each year you let the children scatter petals, forgetfully.
The petals swept at the end of April—
your branches will hold nothing but memory.

TRYST/E

In the small café, walls painted the pale azul
of the train station in Lisbon, I wait for you, then look up
from the children's book of myths I am transcribing:
you arrive & begin unspooling stories
I had been storing deep in my spine.
I apologize for my words, spinning from different time
zones; you ask me, por favor, don't apologize.
That afternoon, I teach you how to pronounce saudade
& the true name of the city where I grew up,
but even in the evening's slow dark, we don't hold
hands, not until late that night, until you hold me dancing—
sweet reward for beating you at darts. This night
is a domino trail of places
you knew, places I wanted to know
you in. When you kiss me
I pull away—¿que pasó? gently, &—I hesitate
on how the word for *sadness* is the same in both our languages,
yet English cannot hold it—
I return to my body in the abandoned games room of the bar & I ask you
if you have another & your *no*
becomes my *now now now*—
now your lips on me, now your arms, now you
pulling me towards you—
Then,
you drive us to those hills where
I see no stars
but pure fog,
though

when we say
constellations,
aren't we only
talking of distances
between already dimming
lights? Espera—
we stay
laughing in your car:
six types of laughter
from me—you
identify like a sonic botanist. We speak
a fresh tongue,
our englishes mix with mimicked
penguin chatter, silly
& in love with
the fog-filled night,
lying till
it becomes light.

And then, we each drive off, headlights on, down the same line on the 101 in opposite directions.

This, I think, is my fado:
to love afternoons turned into morning, and
to love with both hands and eyes closed what is already leaving me.

ELEGY WITH AZEITE E PÃO DE LÓ

—para Tia Madalena, Tio Marcelino, Rita e Tiago

As a child I lived two stories above a funeral home
and I spent my summers on the other side of the Atlantic
Ocean, and I need you to know that none of this is a metaphor.

I need you to know that when I tell you my Tia Madalena
had a voice that sounded like a hundred church bells and
that she washed my hair one July morning with fresh olive oil,

that the olive oil was real and so were her hands in my hair. I need you
to know that this was another language for love— pouring azeite over
a child's head and helping the strands gleam into the summer sunlight.

Words are only air folded into sound and I do not know how real
they are anyway. I am not writing to you in the language my parents
spoke as children. Our goodbyes are even half English, half Portuguese,

a whole other language. What I am trying to say is what I cannot imagine.
I cannot imagine my aunt, her voice a hundred church bells, with lungs
drowning in water that would not save her, a treatment that we knew would

hurt but did not think would kill. I am unable to imagine her breath like that.
I can only hear her voice calling my name *Carlinha* and I think, every year
I am losing someone who calls me by that name, whose tenderness was warm

olive oil in my hair and not merely empty words in air. I am an ocean away
when she dies and my parents go to the house that is empty without her ringing
voice. Tio Marcelino serves pão de ló, a cake of five ingredients and mostly air—

the hands that make it need to firmly whip the egg whites and then gently fold
them so the dough contains enough breath to rise. It is careful work. My father asks,
The cake is good, where is it from? and then regrets asking. Tia made it the night

before she died and I wish this were all some kind of metaphor because then it could
be a bad poem and not a terrible truth. For a child who grew up only a few stories
above so many funerals, I am an adult who is so childish about death: I keep making

this story, that I will go back one day to the home of those summer weekends in Labruge,
that I will ring the bell only to hear her voice filling the air. Instead, we keep these echoes
of her hands, working firm and gentle into a kindness that still cares for us,
that still calls our names.

ST. LUCY'S

To be granted grace in mid
winter by the softness of sun
light breaking the smooth net
work of tentative leaves in the small
space made intimate by benches and shrubs,
by its young trees whose hope rests
in tightly closed buds as water breaks
from the pipes that crawl the brick building is to almost
                                                                                    forget the empty playground.

The playground of concrete and gravel and parking spaces exists
almost beyond notice.

                    The flow of water,
a break-
        ing of the ice upon the pale orange wall,
seeping into pebbled earth, streaming into eroded
bricks as they lie,
          blesses the children's laughter
no longer there,
                                                            teaching the will to stay
                                                                 and the will to break—

FADO IN SEVEN PARTS

When you go to the fountain at the edge of the village this evening,
there will only be the hush of still water and crusted mud.

One day, you will return to the house of the woman
who gave you three silver coins, and she will not be at the window.

This is the house of memory, the tile upon the walls, the dark green couves stirring
in the nearly boiling caldo, São José in terracotta, the afternoon sun gilding the garden.

Watch the patterns of blue arabesque on each tile—
they converge and shift into unreal flowers, bent on journey.

Do not be late, are the words that guide your sandal-bound steps past
the town center, the whitewashed church affronting heaven.

In the middle of the corn fields, green upon growing green, where the mules
bray and the wind carries the cricket movement, you will arrive.

There will be no one waiting for you at the fountain.
The one you wait for shall not return, not from river, not from ocean.

II. COORDINATES

We forget all too soon the things we thought we could never forget. We forget the loves and the betrayals alike, forget what we whispered and what we screamed, forget who we were.

—JOAN DIDION

ELEGY FOR WATER

This will be
for the crisp of you—
the sharp of our need
for your flow.
This will be for the way
you sustained the breath
the movement
the course—
all living things.
This will be
for your clarity.
We, lacking you,
grow forgetful.
This will be a remembrance
of fresh rain,
new fountains,
an ocean, a river, a stream—
What will be the blessing
against
the arid,
the parched,
the de-
hydrated?
O simple gliding,
mystery of polarity,
once gone,
you will leave us
only the salt
of longing.

CROSSING THE LINE

'The girl had a temperature of 105.7 degrees. She hadn't eaten or consumed water for several days But she was detained for eight hours before emergency responders arrived.

The girl had a temperature of 105.7
degrees.
She hadn't
eaten or consumed
water for several days. But
she was detained
for eight hours
before
emergency
responders
arrived.

the girl had a temperature of 105.7 degrees she hadn't eaten
or consumed water for several days but she was detained for eight hours
before emergency responders arrived.

the girl had a temper… f 105.7 degr
or consumed water for several day… ıe was deta
emergency

The girl. 105.7 degrees. water. detained. eight hours.
before. emergency. responders. arrived.

She was 7 years old. Taken into custody by Border Patrol. The Washington Post says:
Guatemalan child entered illegally with her father as part of a large group
crossing into New Mexico.
crossing into new Mexico illegally new Mexico? read it again new Mexico
part of the USA part of you - you say illegally? how do you cross
illegally into new Mexico? how how how [how do you let a child die?]

a 7 year old child died. cause of death: dehydration.
the post mentions she entered illegally.

'Thegirlhadatemperatureof105.7 degreesshehadn'teatenorconsumedwaterforseveraldaysbutshewasdeta inedforeighthoursbeforeemergencyrespondersarrived.

A 7 year old child died for lack of food and water and the newspaper byline reads:
she entered illegally.

look at your hands: now.
remember your hands as a 7-year-old-child
reaching up for a glass
of crisp water.
    you didn't deserve to die then.

A 7 year old child died for lack of
food and water and the newspaper byline says:
she entered--------crossed the line--------that's the part they call illegal

THE 53%

If the word for a gathering of men
  can be called a *threat,*
then a group of white women
  could be called a *margin of error*—
always late to the train, demanding
  passage and taking seats without
reservation. *The future is female,* cosigned
  by colorblind visions in which we
are all women, after all, where white
  women speed past red lights without
incident whereas a black woman dies in jail
  after getting pulled over for a turn signal.

We are all women in our pink pussy hats, as if pink,
as if pussy, were payment enough, in tender.

IN TRANSIT

My bags are heavy against
the weight of the train—
it grates against steel and I long
for continuous days that flow
into one another. Instead
my life is a fretwork of
fragments—strings connected by
inevitable distances.
I am lost in the fury of transit,
writing my poems in a
dark room on paper I cannot see.
Memory bites the new tongue
and I dream of home on a used pillow.

ELEGY FOR DEPARTURE

It's been more than a year now since they gave me the key in that small yellow envelope
that fit within the surface of my palm,

and since I went to open that door, O-24, and it was just an empty room
aching with breathless light.

It was late October and the sunlight
echoed across the room, beneath the arch, sweeping the wooden floor, washing the white walls,

all while I stood there, baffled, with a low-grade fever,
and it took me a moment and then I felt my weight buckle beneath me in an awkward

grace, my knees reaching the floor, my hands clasped in prayer. There was God
and thanks came from some deep place in the pit of my chest. Days later,

I would carry everything I owned across the street
that morning when my friend who came to stay had to go, and that room on the fifth

floor became a wide gaping space between myself and any dream of unity. So by
myself

I took each small thing and arranged my life in cardboard boxes, then going to the gate
still locked to me. That first night

a bitter loneliness slithered beneath the gratitude.
As I sit here now at my desk in a room

that is mine and a place to go, that hot silence comes back to me in the chilled, healthy

light of this different space, and the image rests

and the eager light stays holding the humbled girl on the floor   thankful.

ODE TO A SMALL CREATOR

As the sky deepens into daylight,
his hands sift through moist earth
untangling the undergrowth, the thick crush
of root. There is quiet, a pause of motion,
building the green into his eyes
caught in the tunnel of a microscope,
seeing what others cannot. Shifting
slides of stem cells, piecing together
the fragments into new life, as night brings
itself to what I imagine is a place without
windows somewhere in the heart
of Central Square. Observing light,
he magnifies the smallest pieces—
watch their growth, as even then,
there is a murmur of change somewhere
within the soil of the autumn garden.
Wouldn't each garden choose to be spring
if it could? But it cannot, and now
he measures each drop, each sphere, each limit
to resistance and the calming buzz
of the building echoes his intent—
to chart an entire hidden geography
of origins in this place set apart, where
these nascent cells,
these persistent green buds—
where life!— exists, and he brings it forth
with silent skill.

HYMN

I know you are there tonight in the garden
somewhere, waiting for me,
or rather, I'd like to imagine you are.

I'd like to imagine your hands filled with clay,
gently molding the rusty earth with your fingertips
and setting each curve of undergrowth into measure,

or instead, I'll see you delicately place the pine
beneath the heat of flame, into the blue,
with a knife marking intricate letters in the ancient tongue,

creating a new wordless speech, making it known.
Meanwhile I will be somewhere unraveling yarn,
and placing the strings forward and back between needles.

On a night like tonight when we will be left with no more
words to say, will we be given a way?
Like a pilgrim, I ask now, why did we come here?

Off into the somewhere, somewhere down Church Street,
or somewhere in the garden of the olive trees,
I ask for a will beyond my own, a grace I do not know.

Asking you gently, *do not go, do not go, oh only let me stay,*
I am again at the spiraling staircase, this time in new Carthage,
reading the graffiti gospel: *Disfruta hoy, es más tarde de lo que crees.*

What have we come here to see?
Are we here for the ruins that remain or for what once stood?
What is here stays still and almost standing, a crumbling city.

But like a symbol, it exists.
This is a time before the harvest, before the rebuilding.
I ask my heart to become the root of an olive tree.

LUNULA(E)

Navigators make maps
by the light of
little moons,
crescent moons.

The visible part
of the nail's root
appears at 14 weeks
as little moons,
our fingertips already
beginning to hold
light.

Girls in Rome
wore amulets
of little amber
moons to protect
against
the evil eye,
an eye a pair of
close(d)
parentheses.

Erasmus coined
the term *lunula*
to refer to the rounded
parenthesis,
recalling the curve

of crescent
moons.

The dark of
a crescent moon
is only
what we cannot
see of its
light.

Sometimes we
do not see what lies
in gaps,
the words we choose
to place between
parentheses.

Crescent moons
alight on a path of
parentheses,
a map,
a root,
an eye,
a coin,
calling them by name:
we see the gaps

(   ).

IN THIS POEM, BERT & ERNIE ARE GAY

—for my students

In this poem, Bert & Ernie are gay.
They are not happy in the old-fashioned sense;

and they are not Bert *and* Ernie: they are Bernie,
if you're still searching for their ship name.

In this poem, Bert & Ernie make out on fire
escapes in the city's summer heat, and they

go to pride parades, though Ernie has to drag
Bert there, with promises of porridge to follow.

In this poem, Bert & Ernie get married, and Bert
is actually the one who proposes, with paperclips.

Everyone on Sesame Street is invited and they
throw a block party so loud that the cops are called,

but in this poem, no one is arrested. Bert & Ernie share
an apartment, a walk-in closet, and a bed. They are best friends

with benefits: sex, healthcare, and marriage. They share stories
of people who used to whisper and how they had to play pretend.

In this poem, they are not imaginary. I would know since I made it.
They exist happily, cooing to pigeons in the park and at night, rubber

duckies glow in the dark of their warm and cozy room. In this poem, Bert & Ernie are gay and beautiful and ordinary and they are on your TV.

EURYDICE AND ORPHEUS IN THE CITY

In the heat of mid August, Eurydice
went to rent a flat on the corner
of Broad and Market where the 34 Springfield bus makes its rounds.
She was an old-fashioned girl,
with no particular notion of love
and stayed up late nights, talking with her sister the moon
by long distance.
Evenings, she would call collect, and mornings,
she would take to her typewriter into afternoons
mixed with exhaust and city fume.
Young Orpheus came around and asked her to take a stroll
and she followed him into the underground.
There's gotta be a way around,
he told her, gently, holding Eurydice's hand the way only Orpheus could.
And then he would teach her
to take bird chatter and street lamp light and traffic speech to make song
and her singing filled his days.
He liked to take cherry blossoms and glide them in her hair.
His voice was soft leather when he sang
and his harp was crafted with the finest strands of street echo and passerby threads.
One night Hades, who was never up to any good,
stole away with Eurydice and brought her to the underworld
and fed her salt and dates.
Her tears cried forth the Passaic and it escaped into the earth
where Orpheus swam alone into the river and found a way to the underworld
where Eurydice was knitting her story into knotted thread,
humming an old jukebox song.
Hades gave him one chance to take her back home and he only

had to not look back at Eurydice as
she followed.

He lost that contest.

Orpheus went back to the flat on the corner
of Broad and Market while Eurydice continued to knit
on the banks of Lethe, unsatisfied with the Passaic
which was, after all, a river of persistent memory.

For a while, Orpheus would play her radio in the empty room,
but the wallpaper only soaked up static
so he returned to the streets and took up a new music.

CENTO FOR RACHEL CARSON: A FABLE FOR TODAY

Along the roads: laurel, viburnum, and alder,
great ferns and wildflowers delight the traveler's eye
through much of the year.

Then a strange blight creeps
over the area and everything
begins to change.

Then, the several sudden and unexplained deaths
even among children, stricken suddenly while at play
to die within a few hours.

There comes a strange stillness. The birds, for example—
where have they gone?   Only silence lies
over the fields and woods and marsh.

The apple trees are coming into bloom
but no bees drone among the blossoms,
so there is no pollination and there will be no fruit.

No witchcraft, no enemy action has silenced
the rebirth of new life in this stricken world.
We the people—we have done it ourselves.

FRAGMENTS SHORED AGAINST OUR RUINS[1]

xi. One summer fifteen or so years ago in Portugal, the trees around me are all in flames. Eucalyptus leaves and pine needles burst into sparks. The car zooms through the forest on the one-lane road. These fires are caused by record high temperatures meeting uncharacteristically dry earth. The flames turn the forest into an unreal hellscape. *Close the window.* She fumbles to find the lever. *Close the window.*

ii. *Beginnings are apt to be shadowy, and so it is with the beginnings of that great mother of life, the sea.*[2]

i. To be radical means to get at the roots. The root of the word *hysteria*, for example—

originates from the Greek word for uterus, ὑστέρα, hystera. Ancient Greeks believed that the uterus roams through a woman's body, eventually strangling her and causing disease.[3]

At its roots, to be a woman is to be mad: drowned in moonlight, strangled by a bra.[4] We are always drowning, our cities flooding, our blood flowing. We are always being strangled. They are killing us and they misname it *desire.* They are taking us alive and they misname it *inheritance.* At our roots, we rediscover our origins— radical.

iv. "a spinster with no children" & "probably a Communist"—Secretary of Agriculture Ezra Taft Benson re: Rachel Carson, in a letter to President Dwight D. Eisenhower[5]

---

1 Title is a variation of a line from T. S. Eliot's *The Waste Land* (1921). Original reads: "These fragments I have shored against my ruins."

2 Carson, Rachel (1951). *The Sea Around Us.*

3 O'Brien, Jodi (2009). *Encyclopedia of Gender and Society.*

4 Fisher, Carrie (2008). *Wishful Drinking.*

5 Ed. Matthiessen, Peter (2007). *Courage for the Earth: Writers, Scientists, and Activists Celebrate the Life of Rachel Carson.*

x. I can't imagine men imagining the end of the world in any other way: Eliot's "whimper" or a "bang." When I am studying dead white men at Cambridge, I find Rachel Carson's *Silent Spring*. In a library where they are debating using pesticides to kill the ladybugs, I am in the basement and I read everything by her that I can find.

iii. When Rachel Carson first began the work of *Silent Spring*, the pesticide industry began the work of placing white men in white coats on television to discredit her: "If man were to faithfully follow the teachings of Ms. Carson, we would return to the Dark Ages and the insects, and the diseases, and the vermin would once again inherit the Earth.[6]"

Carson was brought on screen as well, calmly answering questions regarding what her research had shown her to be a matter of life and death, or rather, a matter of many already dying.

She, too, was dying of cancer, already too far gone to recover.

v. "unfair, one-sided, and hysterically overemphatic" with "a mystical attachment to the balance of nature" read one review of *Silent Spring* in *Time*.

Farm Chemicals magazine took it a step further: they portrayed Rachel Carson as a witch on a broom flying in the background.[7]

ix. Imagining the apocalypse in high definition is a hobby for us millennials, fond as we are of killing industries. In high school, for example, we watch the movie *The Day After Tomorrow*. Al Gore has come out with *An Inconvenient Truth* a few years ago and his quiet powerpoint has been quite the sensation. I am afraid for Jake Gyllenhaal, that the wolves will maul his impeccable body, the wolves of course now roaming the frozen hellscape of Manhattan.

---

6 CBS Reports: "The Silent Spring of Rachel Carson." 3 April 1963.

7 Hazlett, Maril (2004). *Environmental History*.

vi. When I cannot sleep at night, I listen to the audiobook of *The Sense of Wonder*, which Carson dedicated to her nephew, though she died before the work was finished. She writes of taking her infant nephew to the ocean's shore late at night, to stare in wonder, unclaiming, finding ghost crabs, and letting the storm move the waves in riot.

What is a witch but a woman men cannot quiet?

vii. In 2019, we receive news that the world as we know it will end by 2040[8]: nearly too far gone to recover. Elon Musk plans to live on Mars and I imagine so does everyone driving Teslas in the carpool lanes on the 101.

I tell my data analyst friend who majored in environmental science: I guess the world is ending in 2040 and somehow this is not a top news story this week. He looks at me, unblinking. The world won't end, he says. It will remain. We will remain. We just won't be able to recognize it. So much of what we now love will be lost.

I am silent as a ghost crab on a forgotten shore.

xii. What is a witch but a woman men cannot control? What is nature but that which we are a part of—"the web of life[9]"? And what on earth are we leaving?

The obligation to endure gives us the right to know.[10]

iix. We don't really know how the world will end. We know that we began in water. Likely, we will end without it. If the world is to be saved, I'd trust it to the hysterical and mystically attached: trees, mothers, moonlight, spinsters, ladybugs, scientists, and witches.

Endings are apt to be shadowy.

---

8 Davenport, Coral (2018). "Major Climate Report Describes a Strong Risk of Crisis as Early as 2040." *The New York Times*.

9 Carson, Rachel (1962). *Silent Spring*.

10 Ibid. Carson is quoting Jean Rostand.

SAUDADE AS LAST DAYS IN TENNESSEE

—for Erin Elizabeth Smith, Jane Wong, and Heather Hasselle

It is not yet dawn, hora da madrugada, and I
am barely waking. All night I have been dreaming of what
Girmay calls "the kingdom of touching; the touches of

the disappearing, things." Already, the morning is disappearing,
rearranging itself into the clothes it wears as day. As I walk
barefoot into Tennessee, my soft soles on wet grass and rocky

earth, my ears fill with the sounds of bleating sheep and a hungry goat.
No one knows where the rooster came from, but he struts, dignified
like a king who knows his kingdom, nearly takes it for granted.

By the door, Simon and River appear as they want to, as they choose,
and they let me hold them against the soft of my body. River tolerates this,
and I know he must be the older, wiser brother while Simon just purrs, purrs,

like this moment is enough for us to keep for a long while, like there is no
leaving for us to be afraid of: oh, this is the kingdom of touching, of what can
and cannot stay. My first full day, I do not write any poems in the way I normally

do, with my fingers upon the keys of my laptop. Instead, I find two dozen eggs
hidden in the corner of the chicken coop, eggs that had been buried away meticulously
by hens with as much hay as they could manage. And who I am to say that is not a poem,

if all poems are, after all, a way of stopping to pay attention to what otherwise goes
unnoticed? Who's to say that Jane and Heather and I standing in the small cabin above
the farm, with chilled rosé in our glasses, talking about love and what could be love and

what was once love, who's to say we weren't all in those moments writing our very best
poems? I am not asking these questions looking for answers, as Tennessee night comes
to call me back, to remind me of my unfinished work. I have spent so much of the day

napping, or as Mary Oliver would say, "letting the soft animal of my body love
what it loves." I fall into these days like rhyme, like a pattern I don't want to break
and I know even as I write, these days are leaving me. But oh yes, they are leaving me

the soft of Simon's belly, the rooster-king's cocksure walk, these waking nights,
and yes even this, even this Tennessee morning.

SELF-PORTRAIT AS A DISAPPEARING ISLAND

In the archipelago
of the dissected dream
lies the quietest
of grasshoppers . . .
there is the munch of words,
the green-leaf crunch of distance,
and the sea walks into

each of our unasked questions.
Sing me that once-learned lull-
aby, rock me back
to sleep. Push the pedals,
steady timing, keep the beat:

Where are you going?
Wish that I knew . . .

Let me remain a while longer an island
without port, without destination,
without longitude and latitude.

Intersecting the ocean,
what remains of land is the archipelago.

The navigators will draw their maps.
The oceans will not remember.

ODE TO THE ISOELECTRONIC

After wiping the rings left by earlier coffee mugs
on the kitchen table, I take this afternoon
in ordinary grace, imagining this one room
to be communal, with its windows
always open, its door never closed.
I set a transparent glass on the table—
it has the sense of something sacred
because it is clear and outside possession.
With unwashed dishes near the cinnamon
and honey, I stir my thoughts into late
tea, sift the remains with a simple spoon.
I am no fortune-teller, not tonight,
and my only understanding of predestination
is that I am given to wander unceasingly
between sister cities, twinning their places
and carrying them like knotted yarn
in my travel bags. What I know of organic
chemistry is that there is a subatomic longing
for synchronicity, for a union at least in mirror
of a structure that is stable, if not static,
that this desire is integral to all these interactions
between shifting atoms, the way we
as humans long for common time zones,
shared rooms, days that follow one another,
and a geography that does not hurt us.

III. ARRIVALS

I am near enough my roots. Time is my friend. Tomorrow is a place we are together.

—SANNA WANI

ODE TO THE SEMICOLON

Small break-
	er and connect-
or, beautiful
	ligament
between
	the muscles of
my thought.
	I crave that bit of
silent music
	only you
can offer—
	the way you
wordlessly serenade
	my speech.
Impossible
	to resist the way
you move.
	Tiny voyeur, I was
once afraid of you
	because I did not
understand you. You,
	constantly present in enumeration,
how many litanies
	have you attended?
Splendid wink,
	clever eye,
you are the keep-
	er of the whole;
you leave nothing un-

attended.
You allow me to believe in con-
tinuity; you celebrate the co-
hesive. You are the break
and the knot,
the tear and the tie.
Small link, resist-
er of fragments,
you give me a breath each time;
opener of spaces in fields
of grammar,
by what power do you move
my tongue,
my eyes,
and measure my beats?

GHAZAL: "AGE OF DISCOVERY"

My ancestors made maps of oceans and lands they
wished to own, traced lines beyond what their eyes could see.

My blood holds the salt of oceans crossed and fishing voyages
without return, bodies lost, still swirling, back to our origin in the sea.

What sins my blood holds from those who tread on land not their own,
whose veins moved with false gospel, nets snarling, killing all they see.

What shorelines call me now, and why I walk gently beside the waves,
hearing since birth, of how the sea takes, does not return, is my legacy.

Discoveries of lands already rich with people we chose not to see—
Carla, meaning manly strength, is dangerous without Sofia, wisdom, do you see?

Discovering our blood holds the same balance of elements as ocean-water—
in mine, Ferreira, meaning iron, meaning my blood, my blood is of iron and of the sea.

MY FATHER TEACHES ME HOW TO OPEN PINE CONES

Place the pine cone close
enough to the fire   not so close
that it burns   there   like that—*assim*

When you hear it crack then
you know   it's time to move
them out   take the *pinça*   not

all the way   not yet   Okay, now
agora, you peel back   each one
to get to the pignole,   you remember?

Espera   I want you to remember   this
that what you put   to flame   it won't
always burn   sometimes   like now see: there are seeds.

ODE TO MY SISTER STARTING WITH PLUMS AND ENDING WITH RAIN

Plums she gathers like ampersands,
connects dreams like crochet, &
still, she—
watch her—
works the day into intricate patterns
of yarn. Her hair falls in
the sway of her
"ands" & "times" & "yes." O my
storyteller mystic
trembling at closed doors,
opening windows to courtyard trees,
greeter of green, survivor of landscapes
where no one ever goes.
It is easy to imagine her,
thoughtful octopus,
ink ribbon-
ing from her mouth
pen twist-
ing in her needle-pointed h
ands
signing a perfect unheard world
filled with times of scrape & hook,
singing into seasons that flow
with cuttlefish & banana slugs,
where everything is articulate in expanding vowels
dipping into diphthongs &
nothing is buried.

I watch her blink & her eyelids hold the sunlight.
She takes my broken shoulders with her child's hands
& turns my down into rise.

Then, she sits by her fire made of ideas & construction paper,
telling me another way to be, rewinding the night into yarn,
daydreaming to me of California, calling my name to tell me there is love,
that we have no more pears, & asking me if tomorrow will bring us rain.

WHEN I WENT OUTSIDE IN A CITY'S APRIL

On the fire escape,
gazing towards the clothesline
that holds taut against the wind—
grazing on pomegranate seeds, I saw the city
move so that the sun appeared to come closer
to the horizon of this miniature skyscraped place,
but now it is still noonhigh heavy spring that feels
with the humid hands of summer, with cars going by, punctuated
by stops at streetlights, small corner intersections, radios letting loose
reggaeton and hip hop and in the street, a mother calling for her child,
a mother stopping to talk to an aunt—whose aunt? they know, those who bother
to remember these family histories—and the neighborhood ice cream truck repeats its
melody in minor chords, out of place, like a witness to a testimony no one called for.

I am still as a small tree and do not sway;
I take my presence from the clothesline
and model myself on small things that grow and do not make noise.

The garlic peppered wind
circles these city streets, bringing
a promise of fresh chicken, Sunday dinners. The train
bounds into the central station and an entire world exists
in there, self-contained against the small community. I can hear
the oldies radio coming from the living room, words that motion towards
those days. The sky changes to fit into the later hour, and I wait upon the hard surface,
adolescent and ironbound.

ODE TO THE EMPANADAS ON PACIFIC & ELM, WITH APOLOGIES TO WILLIAM CARLOS WILLIAMS

Please forgive me, I did not ask the internet for permission
to call it a bodega, the small corner market less than
a two minute walk from the third floor apartment on Pacific,
no less than I was allowed to let my cheeto fuzzed fingers fold
over the pleats of my crisp maroon and gray skirt. In those days,
I confessed my sins to a priest I was not sure would ever see heaven.
How could he? Had he tried the empanadas from the corner market
on Pacific and Elm— fried crispy corners enveloping ground beef
and yet the juices running? Was this not absolution? I believe
in small and human graces: the pleasure of lunchtime
in the crowded cafeteria, the salve of antibiotic on a skinned knee,
water from the rusty faucet after the kickball game on the asphalt
parking lot. Miraculous, those empanadas, and oh *they tasted good*
to me, they tasted good to me. Sorry I—
am not sorry.

ADVENT

Beneath
    what
sterile light
    would lie
a second
    grace?
These days
    hasten
toward winter
    without promise.
Each street now
    becomes silent
with the echo
    of what is not
speaking, not even
    awake.
The river's surface
    nearly frozen,
the dried roots
    of trees
almost emerge.
    At a bus stop,
a mother is waiting
    as the light
rail crosses
    the city as it breaks
between pitch dark
    and early dawn.
Knives in wind

cut corners
as lights dim
in the nearby
suburb.
All is silent.
But so little
bright.

ODE TO THE MAGNOLIA TREES ON WEST MARKET STREET

—for Sister Eileen Bradshaw

Soft violet pink and white—
I thought they were cherry blossoms,
I told the nun who tutored me in math,
but no, she knew those trees,

those trees I watched as I waited to cross
the street to our small brick school on a hill
in the heart of Newark. Good Sister, I miss
the magnolia trees, how they smelled of late March

and early sunshine and cool afternoon breezes,
how simply they stayed, belonged in our city.
When I am all done with my turning back,
retracing my steps through those hallways,

I am left with those magnolia trees—
they stay with me, longing.

TODAY, MY STUDENTS TELL ME

Today, my students tell me that I look like someone
who never drives a car, that I look like I am someone
who takes a train everywhere, and I love that they see me
like this, the same way that I love that one day, a student
asks me, do you buy your clothes on english teacher
dot com?, when the truth is, I would if such a place
existed. Another day, a student tells me that I seem
like the kind of person who is good at tending plants,
that I seem exactly like someone who would care for
dying plants and maybe even heal them, only I am the one
adding *maybe*, because they said it with such conviction
and another student agreed with them like this was simple
and true, and I laughed, told them they were wrong, that I wish
I were more like my grandmother, who was in fact a tender of gardens
and all green things and what I don't tell my students is that I
am so bad at taking care of anything including myself, I don't tell them
that their words, their kindness unprovoked by anything—
like when a student told me I smelled like waffles and they wanted
me to know this was a compliment—this tenderness, even just this shared
nodding of heads, that it takes care of me every day, that it keeps me like a garden.

POEM IN WHICH I CAN SAY POLKA DOTS, TENDERNESS, ICICLES WITHOUT TRANSLATION

Tonight I want to know the word
for polka dots in Portuguese,
for tenderness,
for icicles, the ones that formed so quickly
beneath my car's exhaust today in bitter cold.
In my thoughts, I call you Grandma
though I never called you that in life.
I keep forgetting what it means to live a life
with you not in it, like in the weeks after
your death, I kept waiting for you to call
again and say, just kidding, except I don't
even know how to say just kidding
in Portuguese. I don't even know how
to say goodbye in any language and mean it.
Today I wore polka dots and thought of you
because I still keep your black blouse
with the white polka dots and because
I wore a dress I think you would love.
I would come home and tell you, Avó,
it was so cold outside that icicles grew

beneath the car before I knew it, and I
would be fluent in saying this to you,

I would be fluent in tenderness, and you
would say querida, and my name,

and you would teach me something soft
against the hardness of everything now,

and there would be no poem, only
us in the kitchen, holding hands and warm

bread, I would ask you why you left,
and the wink of your eye would mean,

just kidding, and everything would be without

translation.

FADO: PACIFIC STREET

i still have the key, but the key opens nothing.
—JOSÉ OLIVAREZ

What it means to live in the Ironbound
is to love everything but the traffic.

On summer afternoons with humid air sticky
as a moist lollipop, those waves of heat cover you like a blanket,

as you walk down Pacific Street. At Pacific and Walnut,
John and Marie used to sit outside taking all of it,

all of Newark, all of the Ironbound in, like children take flowers
from tree branches, only to watch the petals fly with nothing but stems

left in grasping hands, and the fragrance of warm flowers lingering on,
calling for more to come, with pollen and plenty.

Two trees reach out to each other from opposite streets:
look closely and you see the branches nearly meet, nearly meet.

Here on Pacific Street, while John and Marie sit on old aluminum chairs,
sweaty soda bottles shine in sad display by the mercado window.

Diamond rings (or so they say) and chains read neon store signs;
hair gets done, laundry made while they rest outside the funeral home,

John with his dark blue baseball cap, Marie in a summer-light blouse and slacks.
Years later, when John died, the loud silence of his keys filled the staircases, no longer

jing-jangling along with his beating steps up into the second floor of the three-floor
apartment home, red brick, green door. On a desk in California, I keep a key

that opens a door that no longer exists, leading into a house of memory
I can no longer enter. Sold for condos to lease, my parents had to move out

of the neighborhood I keep returning to. Now I live near the Pacific Ocean
and still I think of John and Marie in those chairs, on that street, and I ask myself

if it's okay to still call it home.

IV. COMPASS

are you saying that iron understands
time is another name for God?

—LUCILLE CLIFTON

FADO: IRONBOUND

—Ferreira, *from the Latin root for iron*

If by my name, I mean my fate, then it is true
that I am baptized like this city: bound by iron.

Bound by iron tracks in brick city,
I grew up with planes overhead and train whistles in the distance.

Leaving to return is a rhyme we learn as immigrants
and in this city, we sing saudade as thin as the green plastic bags that catch

on the branches of small, emerging trees, roots digging into this earth that is, after all,
mostly iron at its core. We love these streets so much we wash them

with water and with bleach on Sunday mornings before church. In Portuguese,
I love you means *let me clean this for you*, and we show it with chapped hands and old rags.

Iron is a common element of uncommon traits: we find it in our blood
and in our oceans. This city has learned to rust in rain and yet to resist.

Wandering, I know the legend and have memorized it like the prayers from catechism,
like the past perfect tense from porkchop school: I leave, I return, I forget, I remember,

I go nowhere but where I am ironbound.

FADO: SUNDAYS IN MURTOSA

My grandmother's church with all the windows
has widows thumbing rosaries, wearing mourning black.
When their husbands died so did their choice to ever

wear a color other than darkness—de luto, they call it.
Of fighting, I think, as a child walking in, the double doors
creaking open by my grandmother's firm hands.

I squeak in with flip-flops, bright pink tank top,
floral shorts. In America, I am Portuguese, but here
in this widowing church, I am americana, emigrante.

We share bread, the body of the God we worship
in common, but not the language of our prayers.
I move my lips silently and pray I won't get caught.

The calisthenics of mass are familiar: the kneeling
the rising the shuffling for spare change the shaking
of hands only replaced here by a kiss on each cheek.

By heart, I learn to stay awake when the priest's voice becomes
the sound of honeybees in August. I see pious ladies push
each other for place in the communion line, but also, I see

my grandmother, miracle of kindness, fingers nimble after
decades of intricate crochet, holding each bead like beatitude

and I think that this perhaps is the old religion made
new. My hands, rough from climbing orange trees,

hold the ancient rosary she has handed me. I speak
without sound to a God I hope can hear us in this place

IN THIS GARDEN I AM GROWING

I do not know what happens to a body when it stops.
But tell me a story that did not begin in love.
—ARACELIS GIRMAY

Tell me a story of love that does not end in loss.
I am asking you like my whole life depends on it
because it does.

I am trying to grow a garden up out of the earth
in the heart of the city, where the gate is always open,
and you are walking into it.
I like gardens more than
wild places because a garden asks us to tend it, and
in that, there is tenderness. A garden likes to be
kept. It depends on us to go to it. I am asking you to put
your hands in the soil with me. I am asking you to remember my
grandmother's hands in her garden, creating the world, each flower, each spring onion, each
spearmint her way of naming the earth with a voice that was green
and spoke of hot tea with dark
leaves and sliced lemon.

A friend sends me a gift certificate for loose leaf tea
and along with the lavender rooibos, I get a small
packet of wildflower seeds for pollinators. I love that
there are people who are thinking about bumblebees
and hummingbirds and moths and butterflies like our lives
depend on it because they do. I keep the seeds on

my desk for a week before I am ready to scatter them.
They dwell in every possibility of place—

in fact, the seeds hold the future possibilities of a couple
of my past lives: California poppies
and New England asters.
I remember myself in a bar in Bordeaux reading a French
translation of Rexroth's *Autumn in California*. It is spring
time in New Jersey—*spring and all*—and I am wondering
if I can hold it all like this packet of seeds and also if the earth
here will let them grow.

Humidity has always carried the weight of memory
for me, maybe for you too? I would like to see you
face to face. I would like to place my hands across
your face so as to read it by heart. If you touched me,
I think I would break, though.   Touch me anyway.
I am breaking into a new green thing. Bulbous and unwise, I spring
up like the tulips that die first but are brilliant.
I spring up like the tulips that do not believe in death.

Place me anywhere and I am apt to grow roots deep,
except when I lived in a place that was a placeholder for
real places, where cars replaced walking and where I
never could skin my knee on hard cobblestone while falling
from a bike. I have lived several years out like hotel rooms
I rented only to pass the time on my way
to my next urgent destination. Lahiri writes *it is beyond translation*.
Is it?
I do nothing but translate, cross over
continents,
oceans,

and rivers. I am tired
of being in transit.

I am tired of living alone. I am growing a garden
like my life depends on it because it does. It holds
these seeds and I want to believe there will be sunflowers
like the ones I found at the farmer's market in eastern
Pennsylvania one summer. When I think of happiness,
I think of that place sometimes. When I think of happiness,
I think of my feet walking on earth that could hold me
without hesitation and I break open into tenderness.
I, too, need tending.
I am growing a garden
beyond translation, time zones, and transit.
In the garden, I unspool my hair into rhizomes and
my roots grow across this iron-laced earth.

My grandmother is calling me by name,
like my life depends on it   and it does

SAUDADE AS FLOWERS, BREAD, NEEDLE, & OCEAN

Avó, you are calling me back home again—
I am in the garden that you have planted by name
and in the orange trees that hold the sunlight,
and I am your hands toasting the bread in the oven,
buttering the knife, and I am your breath calling me
to the table, and I am asking you to please come back.

Please come back, I am asking you to hold
me as I could not hold you to say goodbye. I am asking you
because I know you would give me anything if I asked,
more than I deserved, so let me be the needle that slipped
while you stitched, disappeared beneath your skin, in your blood,
and is still buried with you, let me be the distance between

you in Portugal and my grandfather in Venezuela for seven years
and let me be a voice saying *no* to your father when your teacher
came to your house and asked him to let you be a teacher when
he said *no*, and you still loved him because you are kinder than
I am, and I am angry or maybe afraid every time someone tells me
how much I am like you because I do not know how to forgive like you
and there is so much I need you to teach me still. You call me back to teach me,

and let me be the ocean you crossed and then the country I crossed and let
the ocean and the country be small, and please I am asking you to to hold me
as you did when I last saw you, let me be the chamomile tea with honey
and the telenovelas and the ginja and the white wine from southern France
you loved   oh how you loved me   and I you
and the laughter and your persistent winks when you told jokes to my English-
speaking friends, and though I know there is another story,

I love the story you told that you chose my name,
I want your name and your voice
in me like the needle, the bread, the ocean,
like the flowers you have named. I fall apart at
the story of how you died,
how you called my name in your last hours alive,
how I could not hold you then,
no, let us write another:

I want the story where I wake up late in the August afternoon, heavy with birdsong,
and you are there, and we
never stop telling these stories—
this is the story where you ask me,
eight hours and thousands of miles apart,
when you will see me again and I tell you, *soon,*

soon, and this time, the story we tell is unfinished
and the story we tell is true

ACKNOWLEDGMENTS & GRATITUDE

Garlands of gratitude to the editors of the following literary magazines and anthologies who provided a home for my work and whose hard work makes community within poetry possible.

Shot Glass Journal: "Notice" and "In Transit"
The Lascaux Review: "Hearsay"
Cotton Xenomorph: "Open Letter to the Boston Blizzard" and "Lunula(e)"
Poached Hare: "In April"
december: "Tryst/e" and "Fado: Sunday in Murtosa"
Washington Square Review: "Elegy with Azeite e Pão de Ló"
Divine Feminist: An Anthology of Poetry & Art by Womxn & Non-Binary Folx: "Advent"
amberflora: "Elegy for Water"
Reclaim: An Anthology of Women's Poetry: "The 53%"
Glass: A Journal of Poetry - Poets Resist: "Crossing the Line"
Hampden-Sydney Poetry Review: "Ode to the Semicolon" and "Elegy for Rhyme"
Off the Coast: "Hymn"
underblong: "In This Poem, Bert & Ernie Are Gay"
Journal of New Jersey Poets: "Eurydice and Orpheus in the City"
Drunk Monkeys: "Saudade as Last Days in Tennessee" (originally published as "Tennessee Morning, Tennessee Night")
Moonchild Magazine: "Cento for Rachel Carson: A Fable for Today"
Honey & Lime: "Fragments Shored Against Our Ruins"
Cheat River Review: "My Father Teaches Me How To Open Pine Cones"
Chameleon Poetry Anthology, a student literary magazine at the University of Cambridge: "When I Went Outside in a City's April"
Okay Donkey: "Ode to the Empanadas on Pacific and Elm, With Apologies to William Carlos Williams"

Grist: "Poem In Which I Can Say Polka Dots, Tenderness, Icicles Without Translation"
EcoTheo: "Today My Students Tell Me"

Several of these poems first appeared in my micro-chapbook, *Ironbound Fados*, published in 2019 with *Ghost City Press*: "Fado: Ironbound," "Orpheus and Eurydice in the City," "When I Went Outside in a City's April," "St. Lucy's," "Fado: Pacific Street," "Fado in Seven Parts," and "Ode to the Magnolia Trees on West Market Street." Warm thanks to the kind and thoughtful editors at Ghost City Press for giving this micro-chap a home.

"Fado in Seven Parts" makes direct references to the following Portuguese fado songs: Carlos Ramos's "Não Venhas Tarde"; Sérgio Nunes's "Lenda da Fonte"; and Amália Rodrigues's "Uma Casa Portuguesa."

"Ode to the Empanadas on Pacific & Elm, With Apologies to William Carlos Williams": The opening is directly inspired by William Carlos Williams' "This Is Just To Say" and the lines, "*they tasted good / to me, they tasted good to me*" are a variation on Williams' "To a Poor Old Woman," in which he repeats "They taste good to her."

The title of "Ransom Note Found Inside A Passport" and style of the poem were inspired by Sandra Simonds' "Ransom Note Attached to Wolf's Ear."

Additionally, I would like to sincerely thank the following organizations for the gifts of time & learning & community:

- Winter Tangerine's poetry workshop at Poets House in New York, New York
- Radical DreamYard Poetry Consortium in the Bronx, New York
- Sundress Academy for the Arts in Knoxville, Tennessee
- The Writing Salon in San Francisco, California

Several poems in this book were written because I was fortunate enough to participate in either residencies or workshops with the above organizations, and I am deeply grateful.

I would also like to thank Arts by the People for their monthly open mic series. Readers, writers, and organizers of this series, I feel so fortunate to have participated in this community. Reading at these open mics, listening to fellow writers, and hosting several of these myself were among some of the most fulfilling experiences within poetry-community that I've had. Special thanks to Paul Rabinowitz and Kathy Kremins for inviting me to host. Thank you to the amazing poets who share their work in this series.

A book is an act of community, and this book would not exist without many who held both my words and me with kindness. The following is an incomplete catalogue of gratitude, starting with my families by blood and by choice. Thank you to my parents, Tony and Linda Ferreira, for steadfast love, carinho throughout the years, for encouraging me to write & to believe in my writing. Thank you, Rosa Malaquias, for not only being my godmother, but also my friend and family: a constant source of support, compassion, and love. Thank you to the Venturas, for making me look forward to every holiday we spend together, for a lifetime of making home feel like whenever we share a meal together, with especially tender love and pride for my goddaughters Erin and Lidia. Thank you to Marie & John Giordano for making 19 Pacific Street home, to Johnny, Judy, and Billy for being extended family. Thank you Rita & Tiago & Tio Marcelino & Tia Madalena—Rita, you always knew I'd write this book, so your name appears in these acknowledgements twice; so grateful for you, more sister than cousin: amo-te muito. Thank you to my grandparents: José & Hermínia Ferreira and Carlos & Domingas Fonseca. This book is dedicated to my grandmother Domingas; vou sempre sentir a tua falta, mas viverás para sempre nestes poemas e no meu coração.

To Newark & its Ironbound, thank you for being my hometown & forever my home.

To my sisters: Alex, Keru, & Siena. You hold my heart & my heart holds such love for our sisterhood. Gratitude for years & hands on shoulders & cups of tea & persimmons & permission.

& to my many geographies & the friends I made there—Cambridge, MA; Bordeaux, France; Cambridge, UK; Los Angeles & Santa Clara—thank you even for the loneliness and the compasses that led me home. Special thanks to Lowell House & the Story-Time players in the first Cambridge; the Oxford Arms crew in Bordeaux; & my Americanists & Bateman Street friends in the second Cambridge. To friends across these geographies, Claire, Aatraye, Justin, Tara, Chase, Daniela, thank you thank you thank you. Paul & Asher & Ryan & Daniel: your friendships have been such light, such joy, such wonderful walks & hot cocoa & matching sweaters & hot tea. Becky, thank you for penguin chocolate friendship, for our walks in city parks & museums & bookstore crawls (across time zones!)—you inspire me as a teacher & your compassion is a blessing & balm.

To my mentors in undergrad, Stephanie Burt, Joanna Klink, & Jorie Graham, thank you for believing in my poems & for being such brilliant lights. Stephanie, your encouragement since the day 17-year old me stepped into your ENG169 class (modern American poetry!) has meant the world.

Gratitude to Saint Vincent Academy as it existed for me as a student from 2004 to 2008, including my extraordinary teachers Ms. Cap, Ms. Piccolo, Sister Connie, Sister Noreen, Sister Eileen Bradshaw, Ms. Palmer, Mr. Hogan, and Mrs. Shiels, and the A-team, Sister June, Sister Margaret, and Ms. Nolan. And to the students I was lucky enough to teach there, thank you beyond words— I miss you still and several of these poems are for you. Marisa, Kelly, and Nicole, I love you and this book would not exist without you three because your love kept me afloat. And Sister Connie, I'm thanking you twice because not only were you an amazing teacher, you became an exceptional colleague and friend—one day, I *will* read *Middlemarch* like I promised you. Mrs. Lim, thank you beyond words for being there throughout the years: your letters were a lifeline; they are still.

My students! How lucky I am, what a gift to have been your teacher—my students in Lycée Condorcet; in St. James in LA; in Mountain View High School; in G-14 at Menlo-Atherton High School; in room 302 at SVA; and across several classrooms at Saint Elizabeth University. My English language learners and my immigrant students, you have my whole heart—thank you for making me a kinder and more thoughtful teacher and human. I love you all more than poetry. I love you across the odyssey and over the garden wall.

Much like my writing cannot happen in isolation, my teaching could not have happened without community. Thank you to my colleagues throughout the years, including those I've already mentioned above. Garlands of gratitude to my M-A crew, whose kindness & solidarity helped me teach *and* write: Cat & Livy & Carrie & Lisa & Liane & Ahzha & Ana & Khoa & more. Cat, you continue to make me a better teacher & better person through your extraordinary friendship; there's never a day when I don't wish your classroom were next door to mine.

Lynne McEniry, wonderful poet, colleague, and friend. Laura Winters, wonderful mentor, colleague, and friend. How lucky I am that our paths crossed & that all these journeys brought me to our cozy English department at St. E's. You both were among the first I told of this book finding a home with River River & I am so grateful for your support throughout: every hug, every shared poem, every post-it of tenderness. Sunflowers in no small abundance to the colleagues who became my friends at St. E's: Adrienne & Stephanie & Mitra & Jake & Franz & more. A.E. Bross and Stephanie Young, the kindness with which you have held both my heart and my writing— gifts beyond the ability of words to thank, so I hope you'll accept my friendship & ongoing endless offers of cups of tea. Joe Ciccone and Anthony Santamaria, thank you for believing in my teaching & making me feel like I belonged.

Whole gardens of flowers & plums from the icebox to the three poets who were kind enough to read & write a blurb for this book: Marina Carreira, Aracelis Girmay, and Roberto Carlos Garcia. Your work both on and off the page has been a compass and a light.

Honey & hortelã to my patient & kind editors, Han VanderHart and Amorak Huey— I am deeply grateful for their stewardship of this book and of this press. River River is a dream, one made real by the labor & energy & time & heart of these two editors. Thank you both beyond words.

Writers who have become friends & guides, thank you for your many kindnesses, in no particular order: Addie Tsai; Stephanie Kaylor; Khaya Osbourne; Hannah Cohen; Chloe N. Clark; Alan Chazaro; Kim Sousa; Zora Satchell; Jared Beloff; Catherine

Rockwood; Catie Garbinsky; Sam Herschel Wein; DeAnna Beachley; Amy Poague; Orchid Cugini; Layne Ransom; Lysz Flo; Kolleen Carney Hoepfner; Devin Kelly; Laura Marshall; Andy Powell; Julia Chen; Keisha Morgendorffer; Pınar Banu Yaşar; Chiara Di Lello; Tom Snarsky; Stephen Furlong; D. Nichole Andrews; Marlin Jenkins; Erin Elizabeth Smith; Topaz Winters; Avni Vyas; Wendy Trevino; Roy G. Guzmán; Aidan Aragon; Wanda Deglane; Gretchen Rockwell; Annie Walters; and Claudia Cortese. Addie, thank you for the countless texts of support & encouragement—steady lights through the fog. Claudia, your friendship has been such fresh wildflowers for me: thank you for every heart-to-heart talk, for your compassion & care.

I have been exceptionally blessed by the kindness of writers & readers. If you helped this book come to be and I didn't mention you by name, here's a caesura for you to write it in:

(& I owe you a poem when we meet in person.)

Moonshadow, you're by my side as I write this—you deserve gratitude, too, dear cat.

And thank you, reader, for your time with this book. I hope it has given you something good, something you can keep, however small, like a city seed or a bit of sea. Your reading of it is a gift to me and I hope in turn, it gave you kindness & garden light.

CARLA SOFIA FERREIRA is a poet and teacher from Newark, New Jersey. Author of micro-chapbook *Ironbound Fados* (Ghost City Press 2019), her poetry and prose have appeared in *The Rumpus, Glamour, Washington Square Review, december, EcoTheo, underblong, Okay Donkey*, and *Cotton Xenomorph*, among others. A recipient of fellowships from the Sundress Academy for the Arts and DreamYard Rad(ical) Poetry Consortium, her poetry has received several nominations for the Pushcart Prize and Best of the Net. One of three students selected to write a creative thesis in poetry during her senior year at Harvard College, Ferreira holds graduate degrees in English and education from the University of Cambridge and Stanford University, respectively. The daughter of Portuguese immigrants, her writing explores transit and transience, urban geographies and distance, tenderness and translation. Her work as an English teacher continues to inform and nourish her writing as a practice of community and care.